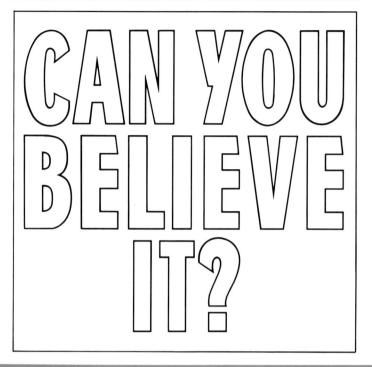

CAN YOU BELIEVE IT?

· BODY POWER ·

Written by
JENNY VAUGHAN

Illustrated by
SALLIE REASON

CHERRYTREE BOOKS

A Cherrytree Book

Designed and produced by Templar Publishing Company Limited,
Pippbrook Mill, London Road, Dorking, Surrey RH4 1JE

First published in 1990
by Cherrytree Press Ltd,
a subsidiary of
The Chivers Company Ltd,
Windsor Bridge Road,
Bath, Avon BA2 3AX

British Library Cataloguing in Publication Data
Vaughan, Jenny *1947–*
    Body power.
    1. Man. Physiology
    I. Title   II. Series
    612

    ISBN 0-7451-5077-2

Typeset by Southern Positives and Negatives (SPAN),
Lingfield, Surrey
Colour separations by Chris Willcock Reproductions,
Maidstone, Kent
Printed and bound by Proost N.V., Turnhout, Belgium

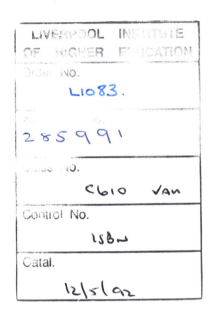

PICTURE CREDITS

Key: Top = t, bottom = b, left = l, right = r

Front cover: b Dr Tony Brain/Science Photo Library; t K. Nahoum/Zefa Picture Library (UK) Ltd

Page 4 Dr Tony Brain/Science Photo Library; page 5 Nasa/Science Photo Library; page 7 Jen and Des Bartlett/Bruce
Coleman Ltd; page 9 Hank Morgan/Science Photo Library; page 10 U.S.I.S./A. Laubier Picture Library; page 11 Mark Tillie;
page 13 Santosh Basak/Frank Spooner Pictures; page 14 Rex Features; page 15 Adam Hart-Davis/Science Photo Library;
page 16 Alan Chandler/Metropolitan Police; page 18 Department of Military Entomology; page 21 Zefa Picture Library (UK)
Ltd; page 24 Alexander Tsiara/Science Photo Library (Inset: Jean Kennedy/Science Photo Library); page 29 Duncan
Raban/The Telegraph Colour Library; page 33 Larry Mulvehill/Science Photo Library;
page 34 A. Edgeworth/Zefa Picture Library (UK) Ltd.

CONTENTS

1. Does our blood contain iron? 4
2. Would we fall over if we had no ears? 4
3. What do hair, nails and hooves have in common? 4
4. Can we drink standing on our heads? 5
5. How tall was the tallest man? 5
6. How long is the small intestine? 6
7. What beats 100,000 times a day? 6
8. How long are your nerves? 7
9. Do we have bones in our ears? 7
10. Do we have as many neck bones as a giraffe? 7
11. How many jobs does the liver do? 8
12. Why are young children 'big heads'? 8
13. How many air sacs are there in our lungs? 9
14. Do we need sleep? 9
15. How much information can a brain store? 9
16. Will eating carrots help you to see in the dark? 10
17. Do our eyes see things upside-down? 10
18. Are your bones stronger than concrete? 10
19. Do double-jointed people have extra joints? 11
20. How much air do we breathe in a lifetime? 11
21. Why doesn't our blood sink down to our feet and
    stay there? 12
22. What happens to your body when you get
    frightened? 12
23. Is skin waterproof? 13
24. If we didn't cut our fingernails would they keep
    growing? 13
25. Can your hair stand on end? 13
26. Do humans really have tails? 14
27. Is seeing believing? 14
28. Can loud noises deafen people? 14
29. Do some people find it hard to tell red from green? 15
30. Are we mostly water? 15
31. How many cells do we have? 16
32. Is it true that no two people have the same
    fingerprints? 16
33. How many hairs do you have on your head? 17
34. Do our brains look like pink cauliflowers? 17
35. Do brains shrink? 17
36. Can a baby hear before it is born? 18
37. Do we really have three million sweat glands? 18
38. Are there really animals living on our eyelashes? 18
39. Is it true that the two halves of our brain have
    different jobs to do? 19
40. How long was the longest hair? 19
41. How fast is a sneeze? 20
42. Do we ever see in black and white? 20
43. Is it true that our tongues can only detect four
    types of taste? 20
44. Is every part of our body the same temperature? 21
45. How much food do we eat in a lifetime? 21
46. How many sperm does a man's body make every
    day? 22
47. Where would you find the Islets of Langerhans? 22
48. How much skin do we have? 23
49. How much blood do our kidneys filter in a day? 23
50. Do our brains send out electrical signals? 24
51. Do babies have to learn to see? 25
52. Can eating carrots turn your skin orange? 25
53. Why do dogs have a better sense of smell than
    humans? 26
54. Why are two eyes better than one? 26
55. Where is your funny bone? 27
56. How fast do we cough? 27
57. Is there an acid bath in your body? 28
58. Is the left side of your brain really linked to the
    right side of your body? 28
59. Do some people have bigger lungs than others? 29
60. Is hay fever caused by hay? 29
61. Can we see things that are not there? 30
62. Do teeth really have roots? 30
63. Why are toes so sensitive? 31
64. How many cells are there in a drop of blood? 31
65. Can you be right-eyed as well as right-handed? 32
66. Are muscles striped? 32
67. Is there a machine that can do the same job as
    our kidneys? 33
68. Do different parts of the brain have different
    jobs to do? 33
69. Do our bodies contain magnets? 34
70. Can we use muscle power to keep warm? 34
71. Are there holes in our bones? 35
72. Are our lungs really self-cleaning? 35
    Index 36

1. Does our blood contain iron?

Our red blood cells contain a substance called **haemoglobin** which has iron in it. Haemoglobin carries oxygen from our lungs to every part of our bodies. The oxygen and iron together make the haemoglobin bright red. When the oxygen is used up by the body, the blood turns dark red.

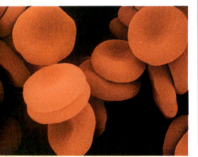

Red blood cells magnified nearly 2000 times by an electron microscope.

2. Would we fall over if we had no ears?

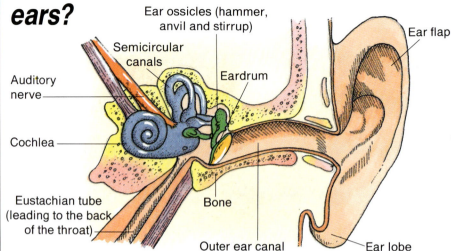

Ear ossicles (hammer, anvil and stirrup)

Semicircular canals

Ear flap

Auditory nerve

Eardrum

Cochlea

Bone

Eustachian tube (leading to the back of the throat)

Outer ear canal

Ear lobe

Our ears have two jobs: we use them to hear and to keep our balance. Deep inside each ear (in the part called the **inner ear**) there are **canals**, which contain fluid and thousands of tiny hairs. This fluid moves whenever we move our heads. The hairs pick up this movement and send messages to the brain. If we are in danger of falling over, the brain sends messages to the rest of the body which then takes action to keep us upright.

3. What do hair, nails and hooves have in common?

Although they look different, hair, nails and hooves are really the same. They are made mainly of a kind of protein called **keratin**. Keratin is also found in the outermost layer of the skin, in animals' horns, fur and claws. In fact, our nails are really just claws which have evolved to become thinner, shorter and flatter.

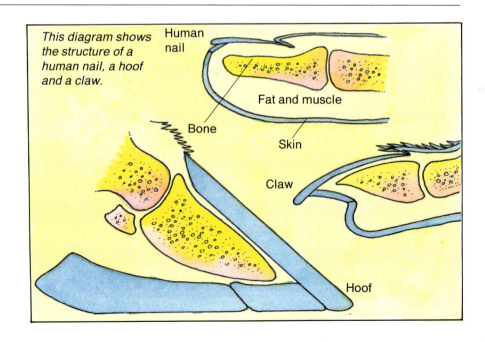

This diagram shows the structure of a human nail, a hoof and a claw.

Human nail

Fat and muscle

Bone

Skin

Claw

Hoof

4. Can we drink standing on our heads?

Yes we can, but don't try – it can be dangerous. Other animals are always doing it – think about how a giraffe drinks! The tube that leads from the mouth to the stomach is lined with strong, smooth muscles. As we swallow, these muscles tighten in a series of wave-like motions which push the food or drink towards the stomach. This movement is called **peristalsis** *and it occurs even if we are upside-down. When food reaches the bottom of the food tube, a valve opens and lets it into the stomach.*

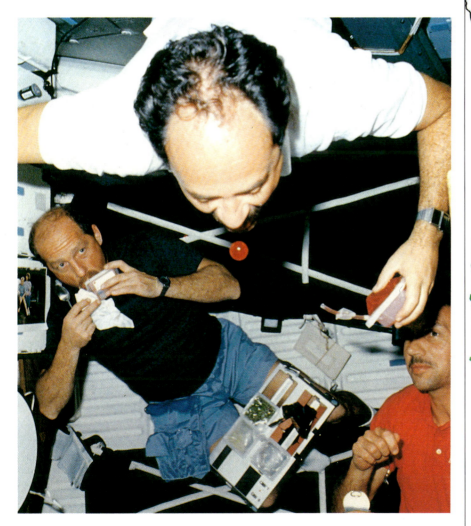

In a weightless environment, astronauts probably find themselves drinking upside-down quite often. In this picture, astronaut John Lounge chases a bubble of strawberry drink during a space shuttle mission in 1988.

5. How tall was the tallest man?

The tallest man who ever lived was about 2.5 metres tall. He was an American named Robert Wadlow. He died in 1940 at the age of 22. People who are unusually tall are often like that because their bodies produce too much of a substance called **growth hormone**.

5

6. How long is the small intestine?

The **small intestine** is part of our **digestive system**. Digestion begins when food enters the mouth. It then passes through the stomach and out into the small intestine. This is small in width (only 2.5 cm), but not in length. In an adult it is about 6.5 metres long. As food passes through the small intestine, nutrients are absorbed and carried off by the blood. The remains pass into the large intestine and then out of the body.

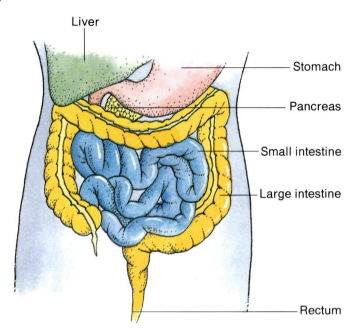

Liver

Stomach

Pancreas

Small intestine

Large intestine

Rectum

7. What beats 100,000 times a day?

The heart does! The heart is made of muscle and acts like a big pump, forcing the blood around our bodies. Inside the heart are four chambers. When the muscles of the heart are relaxed, these chambers expand and blood enters them. When the muscles contract, the blood is forced out of the heart into the blood vessels. Human hearts beat at a rate of about 60 or 70 times a minute. That means there are about 100,000 beats a day. The heart can keep this up for more than 100 years without stopping.

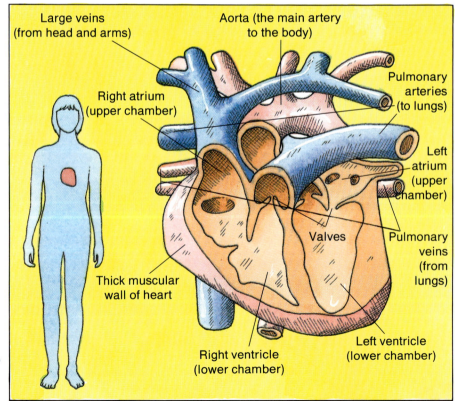

Large veins (from head and arms)

Aorta (the main artery to the body)

Right atrium (upper chamber)

Pulmonary arteries (to lungs)

Left atrium (upper chamber)

Valves

Pulmonary veins (from lungs)

Thick muscular wall of heart

Right ventricle (lower chamber)

Left ventricle (lower chamber)

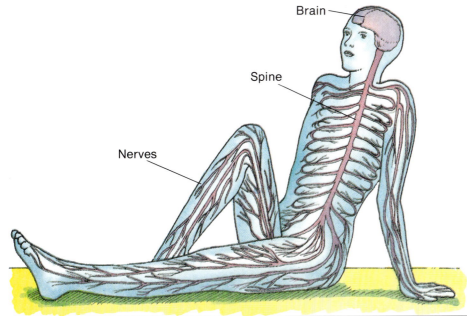

Brain

Spine

Nerves

8. How long are your nerves?

Nerves are long, thin cells, which run all over the body. End to end they would stretch for 75 kilometres. One set of nerves carries a signal about what we smell, see and feel to the brain. These are called **sensory nerves**. Another set, the **motor nerves**, carry messages from the brain to the muscles, telling them what to do.

9. Do we have bones in our ears?

Sounds travel through our ears until they reach a delicate membrane (skin) called the **eardrum**. They make this vibrate. The vibrations then pass from the eardrum along a chain of tiny bones. These enlarge the vibrations and carry them to the inner ear. Here they are turned into electrical signals (see page 24) and sent to the brain.

10. Do we have as many neck bones as a giraffe?

Yes, we do, but the neck bones of the giraffe are much longer than ours. All mammals have seven neck bones, even the tiny shrew. Like other bones in the spine, neck bones have the **spinal cord** running through them. This is a bundle of nerves that carries messages between the body and the brain.

11. How many jobs does the liver do?

The liver does more than 500 jobs. These include storing vitamins, making chemicals that the body needs, keeping the sugar in your body at the right level and processing and storing digested fats. It makes some poisons safe, removes waste products and is a source of heat. All these tasks, and the hundreds of others that the liver carries out, are so important that, without this vital organ, you would die within 24 hours.

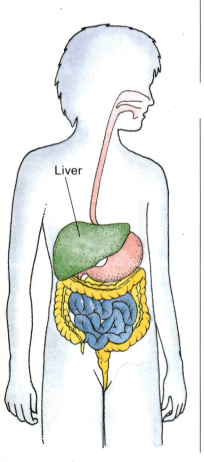

Liver

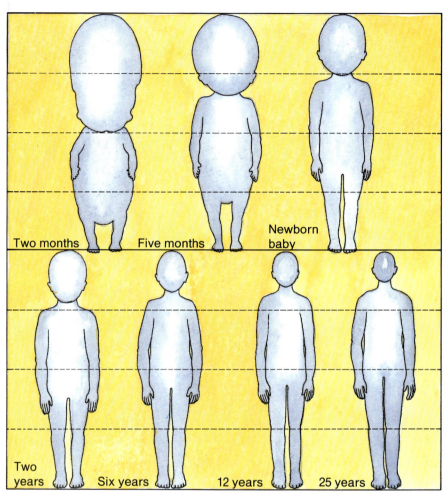

Two months   Five months   Newborn baby

Two years   Six years   12 years   25 years

The diagram above shows the changes in the size of the head in proportion to the body as a baby grows into an adult. You can see that a baby's head grows very large in the early stages.

12. Why are young children 'big heads'?

As a baby grows in its mother's womb, its head and brain grow faster than any other part of the body. When a baby is born, the head is almost a quarter of the body length – about one seventh of its weight is brain. An adult brain is only one fortieth of the body weight. The head remains large compared with the body until adulthood. A baby grows very rapidly while it is in the womb. If this rate of growth did not slow down after birth, it would result in an adult a million times as large as the Sun!

13. How many air sacs are there in our lungs?

Our lungs are a bit like sponges, filled with tiny bubbles, or air sacs, called **alveoli**. In adult lungs there are about 300 million alveoli. When we breathe in, our lungs take in air and absorb oxygen from it. Without oxygen we would die. The air passes into the

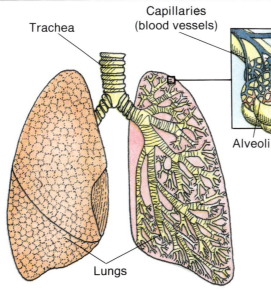

alveoli. The walls of the alveoli are very thin and lined with flat cells which take up the oxygen. From these cells the oxygen passes into tiny blood vessels. The blood then carries the oxygen to the heart.

14. Do we need sleep?

We need the rest sleep gives us, and the younger we are the more we need. A newborn baby sleeps for about 16 hours a day. By the time we are 12, we need only about nine hours' sleep. People become muddled and lack concentration if they are prevented from sleeping for long periods.

15. How much information can a brain store?

People say that the brain is like a computer – but it is much more powerful. A 64k computer can store about 500,000 bits of information whereas the brain can store over 100 million million bits for years and years. This is called long-term memory.

The brain inside this man's head can store more information than the computer he is using.

16. Will eating carrots help you to see in the dark?

Radar helps pilots to see in the dark. It was invented during World War 2, but had to be kept a secret. When asked how they could fly at night, the pilots replied that they ate a lot of carrots. In fact, carrots contain vitamin A, which does *improve your night vision.*

17. Do our eyes see things upside-down?

Our eyes do, but we don't. Rays of light pass into the eye through the **lens**. As they do so, the light rays cross over. This means that the picture that forms on the **retina**, at the back of the eye, is upside-down. But the brain turns this upside-down picture into the one we see, which is the right way up.

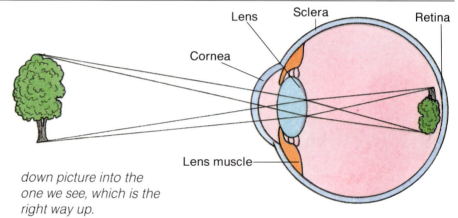

18. Are your bones stronger than concrete?

Bones contain the mineral calcium, which makes them hard, and bunches of a stringy material called **collagen**, which gives them extra strength. Together, these make bones as strong as steel – four times as strong as the same amount of reinforced concrete.

It has been calculated that we breathe enough air in a lifetime to fill two and a half airships! We breathe in about 10 to 14 times a minute (faster after exercise and slower when we are resting), taking in about half a litre of air each time. That adds up to about 15 cubic metres a day. This comes to 400,000 cubic metres in just over 70 years – an average lifetime.

Above you can see the South American contortionist, Hugo Zamorote, demonstrating his double-jointedness. Mr Zamorote can dislocate his joints at will. For the last three years, he has been using this ability in a circus act in which he squeezes himself into incredibly tight places!

19. Do double-jointed people have extra joints?

*No, they have the same number of joints as the rest of us. When we describe someone as **double-jointed**, we mean that they can bend their limbs further than most people, and in more than one direction. They can do this because their **ligaments** (the fibres that hold the joints in place) are very loose.*

11

21. Why doesn't our blood sink down to our feet and stay there?

Blood is pumped around the body by the heart (see page 6). Blood filled with oxygen from the lungs is pumped from the heart along tubes or blood vessels called **arteries**. This blood is pushed along with great force. It carries the oxygen to all parts of the body. On the way back to the heart and lungs, the blood flows through **veins**. By this time it is moving with less force. The veins have valves to stop it flowing backwards.

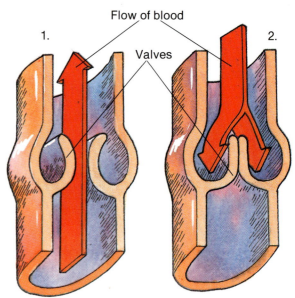

To prevent the blood from flowing backwards, veins have cup-shaped valves. These valves close if the blood changes direction as shown in diagram 2.

22. What happens to your body when you get frightened?

When you get frightened, excited or annoyed, your brain sends messages to some glands near your kidneys called the **adrenal glands**. These prepare the body for action by releasing **adrenaline** into the bloodstream. Adrenaline makes the heart beat faster and stronger, increases the flow of blood to the muscles and decreases the flow of blood to the surface of your skin. Also, the liver releases sugar into the bloodstream so that it can be used by the muscles should you need to fight or run away!

23. Is skin waterproof?

Yes – our skin produces an oily substance called **sebum**. This makes it waterproof. It keeps water out of our bodies when we wash, swim or get caught in the rain. More important, it stops the fluids inside our bodies from escaping.

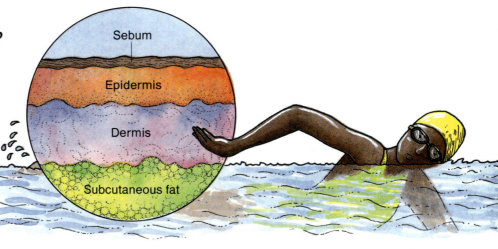

Sebum
Epidermis
Dermis
Subcutaneous fat

25. Can your hair stand on end?

Our bodies are covered in tiny hairs. There is a minute muscle at the root of each hair which can make it stand up or lie flat. When we are cold the muscles pull the hairs up. This traps a layer of air in the spaces between the hairs. The air is warmed by the body and insulates us against the cold outside.

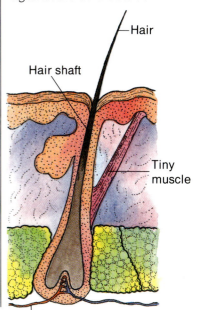

Hair
Hair shaft
Tiny muscle
Blood vessel

24. If we didn't cut our fingernails would they keep growing?

Yes. The longest fingernails in the world belong to Shridhar Chillal of Pune in India. The total length of the nails on his left hand was 426.72 cm in March 1989. The picture above shows Murari Aditya, who eventually cut his incredibly long nails in September 1986. Humans do not use their nails for cutting and tearing, so long nails are not much use.

26. Do humans really have tails?

Yes, we have the remains of one. At the bottom of the spine there are five bones fused together to form part of the **pelvis** (hip bones). Then, below that, there are four tiny bones, called the **coccyx**. These are all that is left of the tail our distant ancestors once had.

Spine (or backbone)

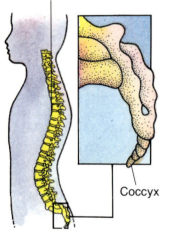

Coccyx

27. Is seeing believing?

Most of the time when we look at an object we know what it is because we have learnt to recognize it. We all know what cats look like whatever their size or shape. Often we can identify everyday objects just by feeling them. Sometimes, however, the image received by our eyes is confusing. Our brains have great difficulty in recognizing and interpreting the picture – then we are not sure what to believe! Such images are called **optical illusions**. Look at the pictures below. What can you see? Check with other people whether they see the same things.

What do you see on the left, a vase or two faces? Look closely at the picture above. To which of the needles at the top of the picture does the point at the bottom belong?

28. Can loud noises deafen people?

Yes, they can. Sound is measured in **decibels**. Any noise above 90 decibels can damage the **cochlea**, in the inner ear, causing deafness. Pop concerts are often above this limit and so is noisy machinery. People working in noisy places often have to wear ear muffs as protection. Sounds above 175 decibels can kill us.

In the picture above, there appears to be a white triangle covering part of three circles and the outline of another triangle, but it is an illusion.

There are two pictures in one here. What do you see? An old woman or a young girl?

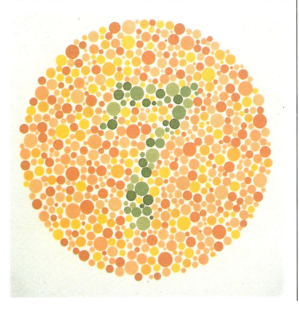

30. Are we mostly water?

The body of an adult man of average size is 60 per cent water. Different parts of the body contain different proportions of water. Our body fluids, such as blood, are mostly water. Even our brains are 80 per cent water. Bones, of course, contain much less. Every day, we lose about 2 litres of water from our bodies, as sweat and urine.

29. Do some people find it hard to tell red from green?

Yes – if there is something wrong with their eyes. At the back of the eye is a layer of cells called the **retina**, which is made up of **cones** and **rods**. The cones are sensitive to colours. If they are faulty, a person may not, for example, be able to tell the difference between red and green. We call this **colour blindness**.

31. How many cells do we have?

*Humans, like all living things, are made up of tiny 'building blocks' called **cells**. These are too small to be seen without a microscope. We have more than 50 million million cells! In the human body there are many different kinds of cells. Each kind is highly specialized for the job that it has to do. For example, there are special cells which make up the blood, the brain, the skin, the liver, the heart and so on. Cells are always dying. Most of them are replaced by new ones.*

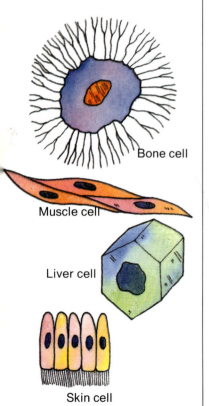

Bone cell

Muscle cell

Liver cell

Skin cell

32. Is it true that no two people have the same fingerprints?

The ends of our fingers are covered with a complicated pattern of tiny ridges. Every person in the world has a unique pattern. The police find this very useful. If a person is arrested for a crime, the police often take a print of his or her fingertips. If a crime is committed, they look for fingerprints left behind on hard, shiny surfaces. These may match up with prints they have on computer files, and so identify the criminal.

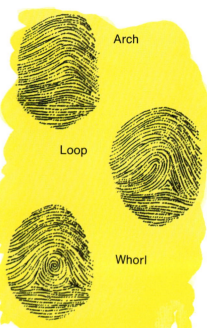

Arch

Loop

Whorl

Fingerprints were first used to solve crime 100 years ago. Although everybody's print is unique, there are three main patterns: the loop, arch and whorl.

33. How many hairs do you have on your head?

Unless you are bald, there are at least 100,000 hairs on your head. Each one grows from the base of a cell called a **hair follicle**. Only a few cells at the root of each hair are living. The rest of the hair is made up of dead scaly cells (see page 4). There are about 5 million hairs on your body. The only places that you do not have hairs are the palms of your hands and the soles of your feet.

34. Do our brains look like pink cauliflowers?

Just under the skull, there is a part of the brain called the **cerebrum**. It looks like two soft, crumpled pink lumps – rather like cauliflowers. These lumps are the part of the brain that controls thinking and intelligence. They are much bigger in humans than in other animals. This is not surprising – we are more intelligent than other animals.

35. Do brains shrink?

When we are children our brains are always growing. They reach their full weight when we are about 20 years old. Brain cells are nerve cells. Unlike other cells (see page 16), these are not replaced as they die. So from the age of about 20 onwards, our brains lose cells and get smaller. Fortunately, we have quite enough to last a lifetime.

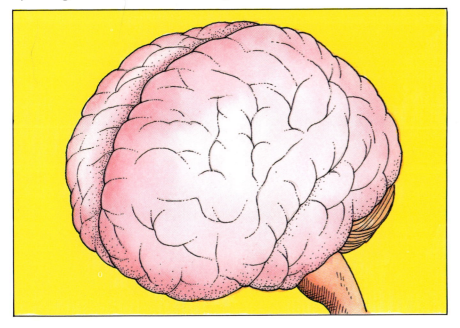

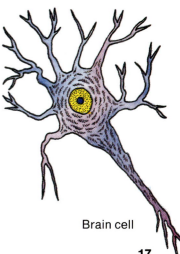

Brain cell

36. Can a baby hear before it is born?

A baby's ears are partly formed only 12 weeks after it has begun to grow in its mother's womb. After six months, it can hear noises which are being made both inside and outside the mother's body. This mother's baby can hear the music from her violin.

37. Do we really have three million sweat glands?

*Yes, adults do. If our sweat glands were laid end to end they would stretch for nearly 50 kilometres. There are sweat glands all over our skin. When we are warm, they produce a salty liquid called **sweat**. This dries and, as it does so, cools the skin. We sweat about a third of a litre a day.*

38. Are there really animals living on our eyelashes?

*Yes. There are tiny creatures called **mites** which live in the oil glands and hair follicles of human skin. They feed on dead skin. They are 0.1 mm long and can only be seen under a high-power microscope. As you sit reading this book, mites are crawling all over your hair, eyebrows and eyelashes! But don't worry, they won't do you any harm!*

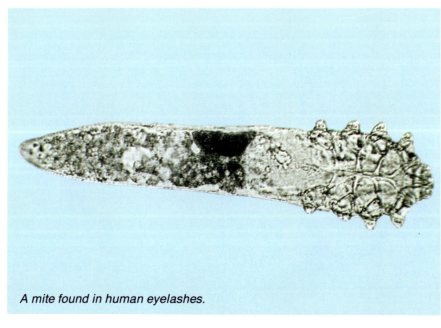

A mite found in human eyelashes.

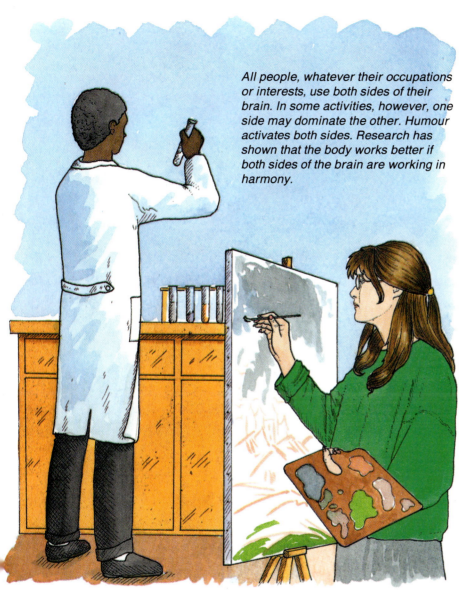

All people, whatever their occupations or interests, use both sides of their brain. In some activities, however, one side may dominate the other. Humour activates both sides. Research has shown that the body works better if both sides of the brain are working in harmony.

40. How long was the longest hair?

It was about 8 metres long. It belonged to Swami Pandarasannadhi, an Indian monk. Few people's hair could ever get that long. Hairs usually grow for a few years and then fall out.

39. Is it true that the two halves of our brain have different jobs to do?

Yes, scientists think that they do. The left half seems to control language and logical thinking. This is the kind of thinking you need to understand science and mathematics. The right half controls artistic and creative thinking. Both halves work together but, for most of us, one half of the brain has more influence than the other. This makes us better at either artistic things or science and mathematics.

41. How fast is a sneeze?

When we sneeze, the air shoots out of our noses at 160 km/h, sometimes even faster. Sneezing is the way the nose rids itself of an irritant, such as dust or pollen, before it reaches the lungs.

42. Do we ever see in black and white?

*Have you noticed that you cannot see colours very well in dim light? This is because the cells in our eyes which detect colours, the **cones**, only work in bright light (see page 15). Another set of cells, called **rods**, enable us to see in dim light, but they cannot detect colour.*

43. Is it true that our tongues can only detect four types of taste?

*It doesn't seem possible – but it is true. We have groups of cells in our tongues, called **taste buds**, which can pick out four different tastes: bitter, sweet, sour and salty. The taste buds send signals along the nervous system to the brain, which interprets the flavour. We think we can taste more than four flavours because we rely on smell when we 'taste' food, just as much as the taste buds. This is why having a blocked nose seems to take our sense of taste away.*

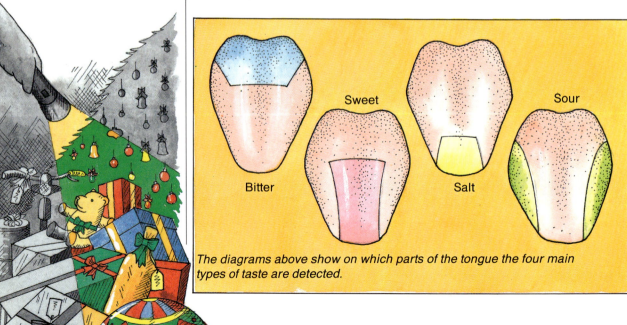

Sweet

Sour

Bitter

Salt

The diagrams above show on which parts of the tongue the four main types of taste are detected.

45. How much food do we eat in a lifetime?

On average, a person living in the western world eats about 30,000 kg of food in a lifetime. To stay healthy, it is important for us to eat a variety of food that gives us all the vitamins, minerals and nutrients we need. **Carbohydrates***, such as bread and pasta, and* **fats** *give us energy. We also need* **protein***, which is made up of* **amino acids***, to make new cells.*

44. Is every part of our body the same temperature?

Our body system is busy 24 hours a day. Some parts of our body are more active than others and so produce more heat. The picture shows what a heat-sensitive photograph of a body looks like. The most active parts are white, the least active are mauve.

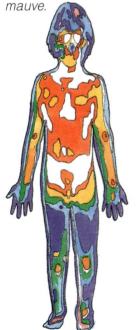

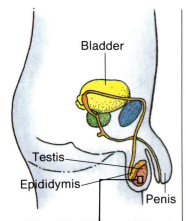

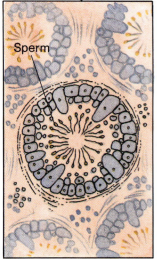

47. Where would you find the Islets of Langerhans?

*You would not find these islets in an ocean, but in your **pancreas**. The pancreas produces enzymes which help to digest food. The Islets of Langerhans are only a small group of cells but they have a very special job to do. They produce **insulin**, a hormone that controls the amount of sugar in your blood. If your body does not produce insulin, you suffer from a disease called diabetes. Too much sugar builds up in your blood and causes many problems. Fortunately, diabetes can be treated with synthetic insulin.*

46. How many sperm does a man's body make every day?

*Sperm are made in the **testes**, or testicles, located in a bag, or pouch, behind the penis called the **scrotum**. They are stored in a long, coiled tube called the **epididymis**. The testes make 500 million new sperm every day. If the sperm are not used, they die off and are absorbed into the body. More are produced to replace them.*

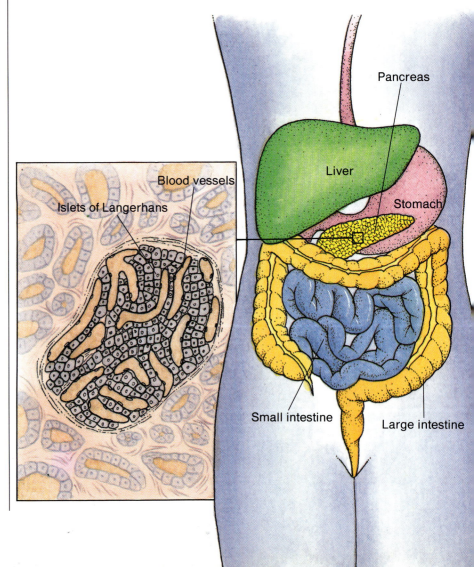

48. How much skin do we have?

If a child of about eight could remove his or her skin and spread it out, it would cover an area of 1.5 square metres. An average-sized adult has about 2 square metres of skin, weighing about 4 kg.

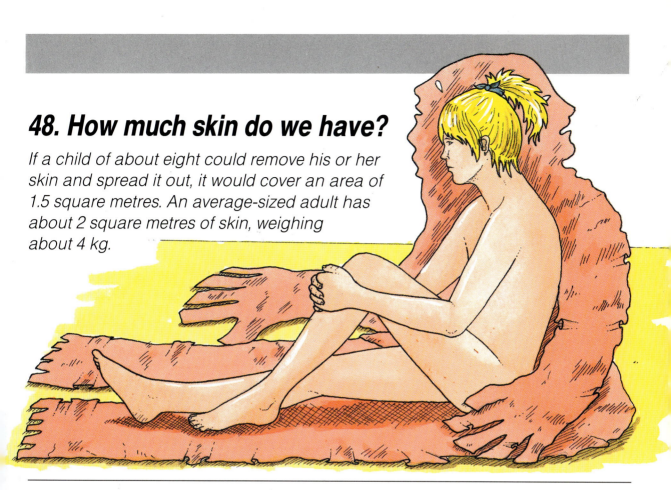

49. How much blood do our kidneys filter in a day?

*Human kidneys are bean-shaped, about 12 cm long and about 150 g in weight. Their job is to clean the blood. They contain millions of tiny tubes. These filter water and waste substances from the blood. Most of the water and some chemicals are returned to the blood. The remaining fluid contains the body's waste products and leaves the body as **urine**. The kidneys never stop working. In 24 hours they filter 1800 litres of blood.*

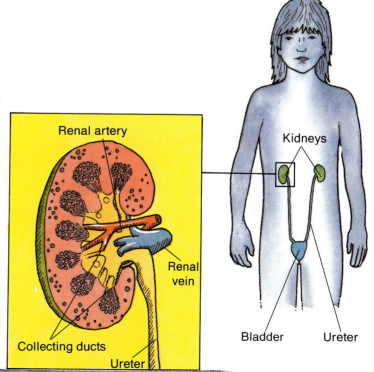

Renal artery

Kidneys

Renal vein

Collecting ducts

Ureter

Bladder

Ureter

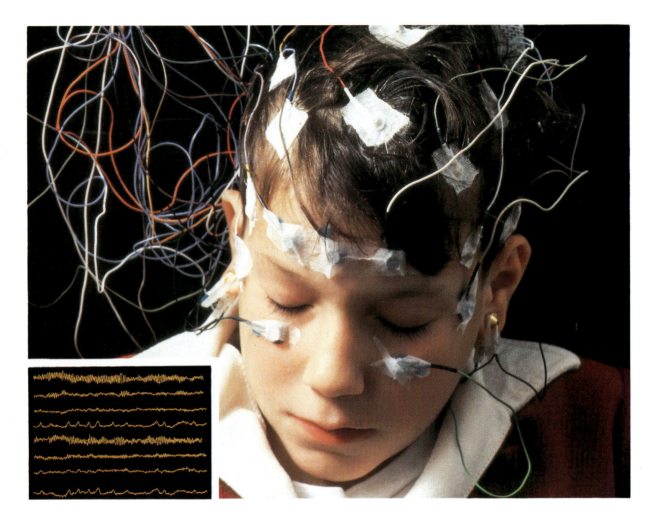

Above: Young boy undergoing an electroencephalograph (EEG) test. The EEG provides a computer with information which allows it to make a map of the electrical activity of the brain.
Inset: An EEG read-out of the brain's alpha waves.

50. Do our brains send out electrical signals?

Yes, all nerve cells produce signals which travel along nerves as short bursts of electricity. Inside the brain, a single nerve may be connected to thousands of others. This makes it possible for electrical signals to take millions of different routes as the brain sends out and receives messages or stores information. It is possible to find out which parts of the brain control which parts of the body. Wires are attached to a person's head which can pick up the bursts of electricity from the brain cells. If the patient then moves an arm or speaks, a machine to which the wires are attached records which part of the brain is sending the signals.

51. Do babies have to learn to see?

Babies do have to learn to see – but it's not something that can be taught. They learn automatically, as they develop. At birth babies can tell light from dark. They soon learn to focus their eyes. After a few months they can recognize faces.

52. Can eating carrots turn your skin orange?

Carrots contain a pigment called **carotene** If you ate a huge quantity of carotene your skin might turn orange, but you might also die. Carotene contains vitamin A which is poisonous in very large quantities.

53. Why do dogs have a better sense of smell than humans?

At the back of the nose there are two areas of cells called **smell receptors**. Each has between 10 and 20 million nerve cells. These are the areas which actually pick up smells. Together they are about the size of a small postage stamp. A dog's smell receptors cover an area 100 times larger than ours.

54. Why are two eyes better than one?

Having two eyes helps us to judge the distance between objects. Our eyes are about 8 cm apart and each one sees objects from a slightly different angle. Our brain combines the images from each eye in a way that gives depth to our view of the world. With only one eye, the world would seem flat and we would be unable to judge distances properly. Our ability to form a single image from two overlapping ones is called **binocular** vision.

The cube is in the area seen by both eyes. Each eye receives a slightly different image of the cube. The brain takes these two images and combines them into one, having height, width, depth and colour.

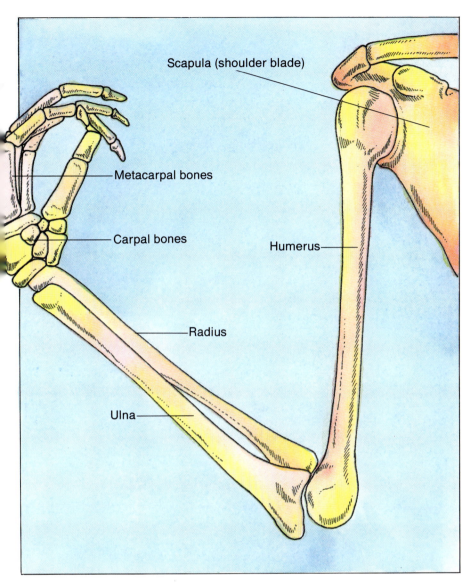

Scapula (shoulder blade)

Metacarpal bones

Carpal bones

Humerus

Radius

Ulna

56. How fast do we cough?

A cough isn't quite as fast as a sneeze – the air comes out of the mouth at 100 km an hour. Coughing is important; it removes dust and other harmful things from the inside of your throat. Before you cough, your vocal cords close tightly and the muscles you use for breathing become tense. Then, suddenly, your vocal cords open and the air shoots out.

55. Where is your funny bone?

Your funny bone is the long bone in the top of your arm. At the top it is attached to the shoulder blade, or scapula, and at the bottom it is attached to the two bones of your lower arm. Some people believe that the funny bone gets its name from the tingling feeling you get when you bang the tip of your elbow. A more likely reason for the bone being called funny is a play on words. The Latin name for the bone is **humerus**, *which sounds exactly like the English word humorous.*

57. Is there an acid bath in your body?

Yes, your stomach! Your stomach is a muscular sac beneath your lungs. It is lined with cells which, when you eat food, release a large amount of hydrochloric acid. The acid helps the enzyme pepsin, which is also produced by the stomach, to break down food. Too much acid can lead to an unpleasant burning sensation called heartburn, and can eventually lead to ulcers.

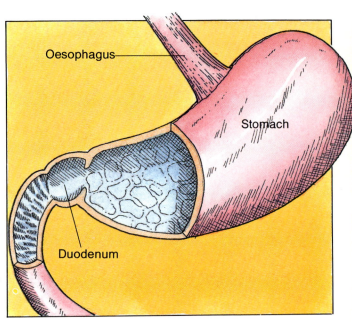

Oesophagus

Stomach

Duodenum

58. Is the left side of your brain really linked to the right side of your body?

Yes, the long strings of nerves that carry signals from all parts of the body to the brain cross over at the base of the skull. Signals from the right side of the body go to the left side of the brain, and the other way round. In most people, the left side of the brain is larger than the right – and the person is right-handed. If the right side is larger, he or she is usually left-handed.

We get hay fever when small particles, such as dust or pollen, irritate the lining of the nose. The body reacts to this irritation as if it were something much more harmful. It produces **antibodies** to fight it off, and this makes us sneeze. It is not just hay, or grasses, that cause hay fever, but many other things as well.

59. Do some people have bigger lungs than others?

Air gets thinner as you get higher because it has less oxygen in it. People who live in mountainous places must have bigger lungs so that they can get the oxygen they need. In parts of Africa, Asia and South America, there are people living in places up to 5000 m above sea level. Lowland visitors to these areas find that they get tired quickly. They become short of breath and their hearts beat faster. Athletes from mountainous regions often have an advantage over lowland competitors. Their large lungs help them get extra oxygen while they are running at lower altitudes.

61. Can we see things that are not there?

Sometimes people think they can – but it's usually a sign that something is wrong. It happens when the brain acts as if it were getting signals from the eyes, when, in fact, the signals are coming from within the mind. We call these false images **hallucinations**. Some kinds of illness, some drugs and lack of sleep can cause them.

62. Do teeth really have roots?

A tooth has three main parts: the crown, the neck and the root. The crown is the part that sticks out of the gum. It is covered with hard **enamel** which protects the tooth as we bite and chew. The root is held in the bone of the jaw by a strong ligament. Inside the tooth is the part known as the **pulp**. This contains nerves and blood vessels which connect with the blood stream.

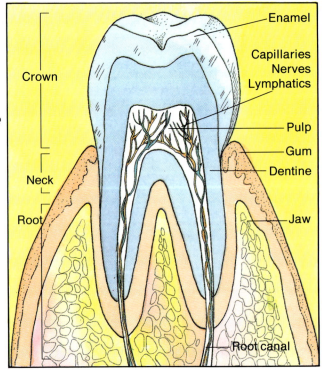

Crown

Enamel

Capillaries
Nerves
Lymphatics

Pulp

Gum

Neck

Dentine

Root

Jaw

Root canal

63. *Why are toes so sensitive?*

Before swimming, you test how cold the water is with the tips of your toes. This is because they are very sensitive – they have a large number of sensory nerve endings (see page 7). Other parts of the body are also highly sensitive – your lips, tongue or fingers, for example. The little man pictured below is called an **homunculus**. *The diagram shows the parts of the body that are the most sensitive. The parts of the brain that control these sensitive areas are larger than the parts controlling less sensitive areas of the body.*

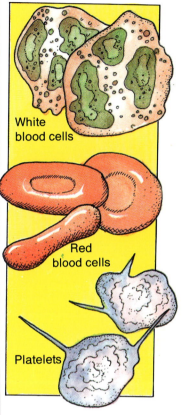

White blood cells

Red blood cells

Platelets

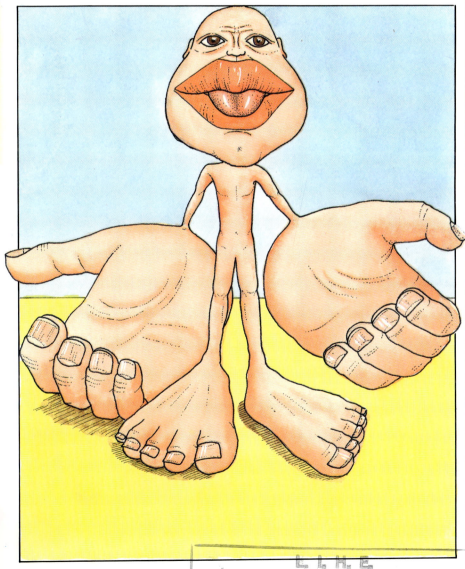

64. *How many cells are there in a drop of blood?*

In a drop of blood only the size of a pin-head, there could be 5 million **red blood cells**. *These carry oxygen around the body. There could also be about 10,000* **white blood cells**. *These are much bigger than red ones, and help us to fight infection. There are about 250,000* **platelets**, *which help the blood clot when we cut ourselves.*

65. Can you be right-eyed as well as right-handed?

*Yes. We all have a **dominant eye**. Which eye it is depends on whether our brain is left- or right-sided (see page 28). To find out which of your eyes is dominant, do the following experiment. Make a circle with your thumb and forefinger. Hold this out in front of you and, with both your eyes open, look through it at a distant object. Now close one eye and look at the object. Repeat this with the other eye. You will only be able to see the object through the circle with one of your eyes. That is your dominant eye. Is it the same as your dominant hand?*

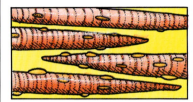
Striated, or striped, muscle

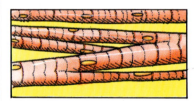
Cardiac muscle

Smooth muscle

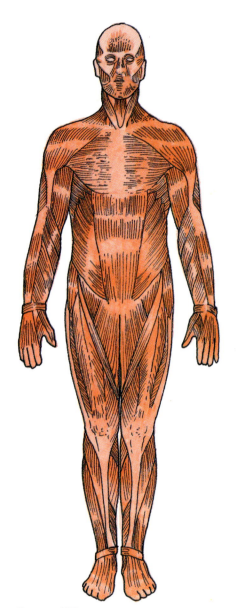

66. Are muscles striped?

*Some of our muscles are **striated**, or striped. These are the **skeletal** muscles – the ones we can control and which make it possible for us to move our bodies. They are striped because the fibres that make up the muscles contain two different kinds of protein. These are not the only kind of muscle we have. Other kinds are the **cardiac** muscles (heart muscles) which look less striped than skeletal muscles, and **smooth** muscles, which are not striped at all. These help our internal body systems to work properly.*

67. Is there a machine that can do the same job as our kidneys?

*There are machines that people use if their kidneys do not work or have been removed. These are called **kidney dialysis machines**. A tube carries the blood from the person's body through a filtering system, which removes waste products. If these were not removed, they could endanger the person's life. Two or three overnight sessions a week, at home or in a hospital, are usually enough to purify the blood.*

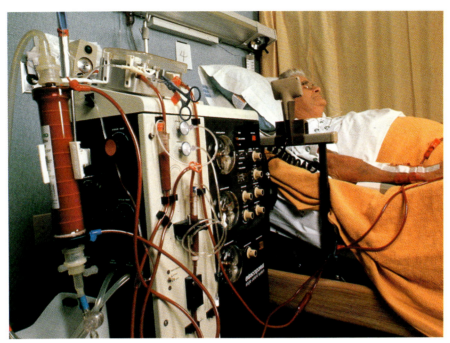

Patient undergoing treatment on a kidney dialysis machine.

68. Do different parts of the brain have different jobs to do?

*Yes, they do. The large outside **cortex**, or **cerebrum**, is where we do our thinking. The picture shows where in the brain the different activities of our bodies are controlled. Beneath the cerebrum, there are other parts of the brain. The **medulla** controls activities that we do not have to think about, such as breathing. The **cerebellum** controls our sense of balance and the actions we do think about, such as writing or kicking a ball.*

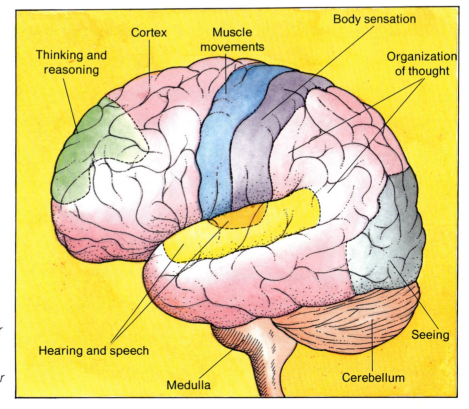

69. Do our bodies contain magnets?

It appears that we have magnetic tissue just behind our noses. Experiments have shown that blindfolded people taken to an unfamiliar area are more likely to find their way back home than people without a blindfold. They do so 'using' their internal compass.

70. Can we use muscle power to keep warm?

When we take exercise, we use our muscles. As we do this, the muscles use energy from the food we have digested. As they work, the muscles release energy in the form of heat, and we feel warmer. The harder we work our muscles, the more energy we need and the warmer we get. We need more oxygen, too, which is why we pant and why our hearts work harder, pumping more blood around our bodies.

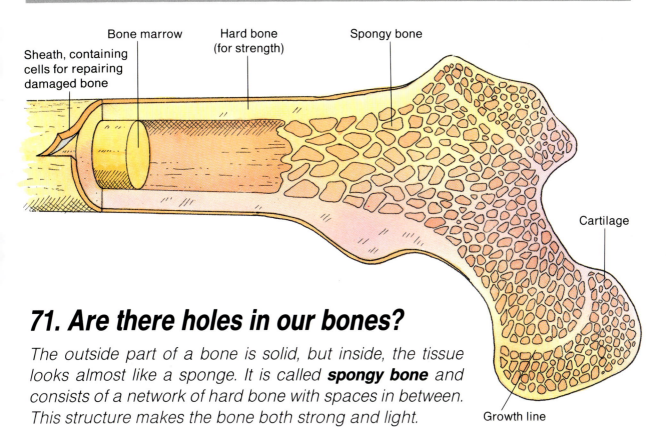

Sheath, containing cells for repairing damaged bone

Bone marrow

Hard bone (for strength)

Spongy bone

Cartilage

Growth line

71. Are there holes in our bones?

The outside part of a bone is solid, but inside, the tissue looks almost like a sponge. It is called **spongy bone** *and consists of a network of hard bone with spaces in between. This structure makes the bone both strong and light.*

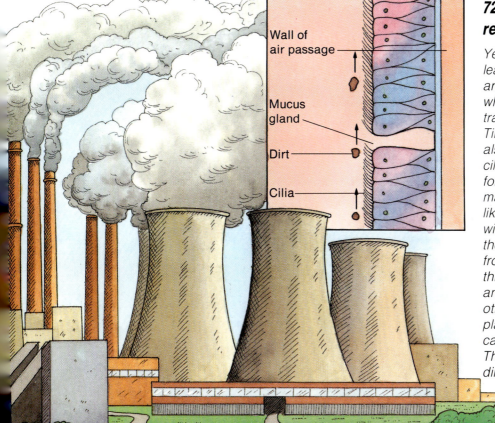

Wall of air passage

Mucus gland

Dirt

Cilia

72. Are our lungs really self-cleaning?

Yes, or at least the tubes leading into our lungs are. The sticky mucus which lines these tubes traps dirt from the air. Tiny hairs called **cilia** *also line the tubes. The cilia beat backwards and forwards in the mucus, making waves in it – a bit like grass blowing in the wind. The waves carry the dirt upwards, away from the lungs to the throat. People who live and work in dusty or otherwise polluted places, or who smoke, can damage their lungs. The cilia stop working as dirt builds up.*

INDEX

acid 28
adrenal glands 12
adrenaline 12
alveoli 9
amino acids 21
antibodies 29
arteries 6, 12

babies 8, 9, 18, 25
binocular vision 26
blood 4, 6, 9, 12, 15, 16, 23, 31, 33
body fluids 15
bones 10, 14, 15, 27, 35
brain 4, 7, 8, 9, 12, 14, 15, 16, 17, 19, 24, 26, 28, 30, 31, 32, 33
breathing 9, 11, 33

capillaries 9
carbohydrates 21
cells 4, 7, 9, 15, 16, 17, 20, 21, 22, 24, 26, 28, 31
cerebrum 17, 33
cilia 35
claws 4
coccyx 14
cochlea 14
colour blindness 15
cones 15, 20
cornea 10
cortex 33

deafness 14
decibels 14
digestive system 6
duodenum 28

ears 4, 7, 18
electrical activity 24
enamel 30
epididymis 22
eyelashes 18
eyes 10, 14, 15, 26, 30, 32

fats 8, 21
feet 17
fingers 16, 31
follicles 17, 18
food 5, 6, 21, 22, 34
fur 4

growth 5, 8

haemoglobin 4
hair 4, 13, 17, 18, 19
hallucinations 30
hands 17
hay fever 29
head 4, 8, 17, 24
hearing 14, 18
heart 6, 12, 34

heat 21, 34
homunculus 31
hooves 4
humerus 27

insulin 22
intestines 6
Islets of Langerhans 22

joints 11

keratin 4
kidney dialysis 33
kidneys 12, 23, 33

lens 10
ligaments 11
lips 31
liver 6, 8, 12, 16
lungs 4, 9, 12, 20, 28, 29, 35

mites 18
mouth 5, 6
muscles 5, 6, 7, 12, 13, 32, 34

nails 4, 13
neck 7
nerves 7, 24, 28
nose 26, 34
nutrients 6, 21

oesophagus 28
oil glands 18
optical illusions 14
oxygen 4, 9, 12, 29, 34

pancreas 6, 22
pelvis 14
penis 22
peristalsis 5
platelets 31
protein 4, 21, 32
pulp 30

rectum 6
red blood cells 4, 31
retina 10, 15
rods 15, 20

scapula 27
scrotum 22
sebum 13
sight 10, 14, 15, 20, 25, 26
skin 4, 12, 13, 16, 18, 23
skull 17, 28
sleep 9, 30
smell receptors 26
sneezing 20, 27, 29
sounds 14, 18
sperms 22

spinal cord 7
spine 7, 14
spongy bone 35
stomach 5, 6, 28
sugar 8, 12, 22
sweat 15, 18

taste buds 20
teeth 30
testes 22
toes 31
tongue 20, 31
touch 14, 31
trachea 9

urine 15, 23

veins 6, 12
vitamins 8, 10, 21, 25
vocal chords 27

white blood cells 31
womb 8, 18